Spoken Words Fly Away, Written Words Remain

poems by

Lauren Lewis

Finishing Line Press
Georgetown, Kentucky

Spoken Words Fly Away, Written Words Remain

For my family. Thank you for letting me share these moments with you.

Copyright © 2019 by Lauren Lewis
ISBN 978-1-64662-060-9 First Edition
All rights reserved under International and Pan-American Copyright Conventions. No part of this book may be reproduced in any manner whatsoever without written permission from the publisher, except in the case of brief quotations embodied in critical articles and reviews.

Publisher: Leah Maines

Editor: Christen Kincaid

Cover Art: Lauren Lewis

Author Photo: Lauren Lewis

Cover Design: Elizabeth Maines McCleavy

Printed in the USA on acid-free paper.
Order online: www.finishinglinepress.com
also available on amazon.com

Author inquiries and mail orders:
Finishing Line Press
P. O. Box 1626
Georgetown, Kentucky 40324
U. S. A.

Table of Contents

forget-me-nots 1
eleven days of unshaded sun.. 2
$6CO_2 + 6H_2O \rightarrow C_6H_{12}O_6 + 6O_2$ 3
"She held her heart in her hands"...................................... 4
"A fire rages on the eastern horizon"................................ 5
four blue eggs 6
"I can hear the baby birds" 7
"If you've ever seen a baby bird" 8
"I would very much like to meet the man" 9
"That pink July rain"... 10
"The wrought-iron rods" 11
poetry: poe-eh-tree 12
Annabeth Brown 13
"I like to watch the hawk soar" 14
prisoner to the sky.. 15
Endangered Eyes... 16
Endure.. 17
Chain-Link Fence.. 18
That freckle in your eye 19
a murder 20
I wanna lie on an old faded blanket 21
"there's something about a blue sky".............................. 22
"the wind breathes life into waves of " 23
My father is a tree 24
"Swollen hands"...25
May the Trees Bear Witness...26
Eggs 27
Glass Eyes 28
The Weight of the Rain.. 29
The Future Is Ours.. 30
there is no such thing as silence 31
"The sunshine passes unfiltered".................................... 32
"I want to taste the blue".. 33
"The sun slips below the horizon" 34
Uranus has 21 moons... 35
a sleeping forest.. 36

forget-me-nots

a seed
small and brown
i could hold a thousand
in my left hand
but only six make it into the plastic pot
forget-me-nots, the package says
a small, blue flower, thirsty
they enjoy partial sun and shade
i wonder how they like
my chilly windowsill
the sun's early light from the east
that slants through the frosty windowpane
the purified rain from my brita water bottle
apparently they feel quite at home
as they have left their brown shells
transformed into thin green stems
with two leaves each, reaching
past the glass,
toward the cerulean sky

eleven days of unshaded sun

arid air with no relief
for their burning thirst

the warm light
once gentle and giving
turned angry and harsh

the cool ledge where they rested
became a solar sauna
with no place to go
and no way to get there

they grew thin and frail
weak and withered
they collapsed
empty
skin burned and wrinkled

no amount of water
or love
could bring them back

the flowers on the windowsill
were dead

$$6CO_2 + 6H_2O \rightarrow C_6H_{12}O_6 + 6O_2$$

A dark veil is lifted.
The sun pirouettes
across an azure curtain,
the stage coming to life
beneath her.

Green leaves grow
translucent under her spotlight.

Their dark veins
slither sensually,
seducing the wind
as they twirl and thrash,
churning in the air, absorbing
the audience's declarations of delight.

They drink in the tears
of cascading condensation
shed by the atmosphere.

Mixed with the sun's praise
they slow to concoct a sweet energy
ending on a sigh
of pure air, and
finally growing still.

With a final turn,
the sun vanishes off
the edge of the stage.

She held her heart in her hands,
a glass jar
filled with fireflies.

Outstretched and waiting
for you to take it,
but you didn't.

And it grew heavy in her hands
until it slipped through her fingers
and – shattered – on the floor.

Leaving her with nothing more
than shards of broken glass
and the blood of a thousand fireflies.

A fire rages on the eastern horizon.
A bloody inferno ignited by
the sun's revival.
It consumes the clouds;
they didn't stand a chance
against the fleeting flames
that licked the sky
before being extinguished
by a blanket of blue:
a balm to soothe the burn
of dawn.

four blue eggs

obsessed
I check the nest
every day
the heat of summer
under the eaves
and their mother's crimson breast
transforms four blue eggs
into ancient dinosaurs
skin as wrinkled and red as
a sun-withered chili pepper
all beak and bulbous eyes
just a tuft of downy at their crown
mouths stuck open
waiting
how they lift their heads with that
scrawny neck
I will never know

I can hear the baby birds
chirping, their bellies
empty, waiting
for mama to return
with breakfast

I see her
watching me,
waiting
for me to leave,
lest I discover
her clever nesting place
in the wooden house
atop a metal pole
in my backyard.

If you've ever
seen a baby bird
fly for the first
time, you might
smile as he perches
on the edge of
his nest, then changes
his mind and goes back
to the comfort of
what he knows is
safe. And smile once
more when he is
feeling brave again
tottering on the edge
indecision in his eyes.
You might gasp
when you watch
him leap, or rather
free fall and flap
his weak wings
furiously, trying to
stay airborne
as he slowly sinks
to the ground.
You might rush
to his aid, hoping to
save him from
himself, only to find,
once you get there
that he is already

gone.

I would very much
like to meet the man
who resides just beyond the horizon
and spends the lighted hours
imagining and planning
a new masterpiece.
The one who holds the brush,
flitting from shadow to shadow,
and paints for us,
with only the light of the stars,
the definition of beauty
each morning
and then retreats before
anyone can praise him for it.

That pink July rain
came down so cool
that summer afternoon.

The garden drank
and drank the
sweet, delicate drops

that pitter-pattered
off the roof.

And that empty
porch swing
swayed noiselessly
on well-oiled chains

as we ran
barefoot
through the slick grass
and pretended we could fly.

The wrought-iron rods
stand strong underneath
the blazing sun,
hot to the touch.
Through the bars
I watch the elephant
sway in his cage
back and forth,
back and forth.
Water trickles by
in a man-made stream
whose basin is far too blue.
The elephant's eyes
nearly lost beneath
wrinkled lips, sweep
left to right,
left to right.
The sounds of nature
sound more like static.
The elephant
lifts his leg
and sets it down,
lifts his leg
and sets it down.
The single tree's
paint is fading
as it stands
silent and still
in the wind,
while the elephant slowly
shakes his head
back and forth,
back and forth.

poetry

poe-eh-tree
noun

the art of using
pretty words
imaginative adjectives and
figures of speech
to turn the plainest weed
into the most exotic flower
you have ever seen

Annabeth Brown

When she was
6, she told them
she was a baby

Robin. I came from
a pretty blue egg
she said.

They smiled
and said of course
you did, you

pretty little bird.
She would whistle
sweet soft songs

and flit here and there
flapping her stick-skinny
arms as smooth and

featherless as a stone
spun for miles
by a raging river.

Then one day she
climbed the wooden
trellis and pulled

herself up onto
the garage's aging
roof. Her barefoot toes

gripped the edge
tightly. And as the wind
picked up, she threw

wide her arms and closed
her Robin's egg blue
eyes, convinced she could

fly.

I like to watch
the hawk soar.
Weathered wings spread
but not flapping.
Body buoyant on the breeze,
weightless,
suspended in time,
a silent snapshot
of a forgotten moment
that you only remember
when the sun shines
through the trees
a certain way.

prisoner to the sky

i explore the stars
live in the breeze
dance on the blue air
linger in the secrets
of the clouds
heart longing only
for someone to fly with

Endangered Eyes

Windows into the soul,
survivors,
the last of their kind.
Empty irises of hope.
Broken hearts that remind
us of broken promises defined
by the cries
that nobody hears
because they're all
gone.

Endure

That old peach tree
still stands,
crooked now,
in the field
with knotted branches
and gnarled knuckles
matching the man's
who still picks
the velvet fruit
for his love
every day.

Chain-Link Fence

Dirty fingers trail across cool metal
as the sun burns the ground below
and heat rises in disorienting waves from the blacktop.
No wind blows to cool flushed skin,
too hot, even for the cicadas.

The once green grass lies shriveled and dead.
Nothing to see but air.
Nothing to hear but the sun.
Nothing to smell but silence.
Nothing to taste but heat.
Nothing to feel but the cool metal links of an ever-present fence beneath dirty fingers
and the first drop of rain from a cloudless sky.

That freckle in your eye

A fleck of gold
basking in a pool
of melted African jade
rimmed with a circlet of dark green garnet.

A hidden treasure
that found its haven
in your left iris.

Safe from the greedy
clutching hands of strangers.

Known only to those
who lean in close enough

to kiss.

a murder:

they gather,
coal black, and flutter
in the inky darkness
of a starless sky.

onyx eyes peer
out of murky air.

screaming,
tongues stained crimson,
they turn and fly
into the void
left by the moon.

I wanna lie

on an old faded blanket
and stare up at the stars
when they don't have to
compete with the city lights
to see who can shine
the brightest

I wanna sip
homemade hot chocolate
with too many marshmallows
from an old steel thermos
as I watch them dance
across a near black sky

I wanna hold someone's
strong hand in mine,
listen to the song of the stars
and find out what they mean
when they sing about
true love.

there's something about
a blue sky
unmarred by cottony clouds
or wispy trails of planes
that makes the blood in my veins
race like a spring breeze
a vibrant velocity
strong enough
to lift my heart
a pink, plastic kite,
a painted, soaring eagle
in flight

the wind breathes life into waves of
ghostly green grass
waist-high, the waterless sea
whispers my name
the undulating knolls rip and roll
a titillating tide
a cascading caress
calling me home

My father

is a tree. He has
strong branches that can support
his struggles. His trunk is solid and firm. When
the fall comes,
as it does once a year, he struggles to hold on to
his leaves. Some
fall sooner than others. Eventually they all leave,
but
he never falters. In
the winter,
his brown
bark is
bare
and
cold.
But the
spring
returns,
and with
it, his
leaves—
and his smile.

Swollen hands, fingers fat with arthritis,
he scrubs them mercilessly with steaming water
and dishwasher soap.
An oil-slicked duckling slips and slides on
a rainbow beach.
Why don't they ever come clean? I ask.
Maybe I'm not scrubbing hard enough, he says.
Maybe I need some gasoline.

May the Trees Bear Witness

The leaves drift silently to the cold ground,
reds, oranges, yellows and some brown.
They land softly on the thickly covered, wet floor.
The now bare Trees shiver, cold to their core.
A chill wind whispers through the evergreens, kissed,
as dawn approaches, with a still frozen mist.
A Doe and Fawn emerge, unnoticed and unhindered;
but danger was something they always considered.

They walk silently, together, through the thin Trees.
Her ears prick up; she heard a noise on the breeze.
Body tense, her eyes scan the cold darkness.
A trick of the wind, it was probably harmless.
The sun broke through the Trees as they reached a steaming stream.
They drank the crisp water and, through the stillness, an arrow screamed.
Through the silence and Trees it quickly flew.
Unstoppable and sharp, its aim was true.
The hunter approached from the Trees up ahead,
as the Doe sank in the water, an arrow in her chest. Dead.
The trees watched, empty, they had no tears to shed.
And the Fawn watched from the far bank as the once clear water ran red.

Eggs

He pulled into the drive after a half day at the office.
Home early to a wife who was gorgeous, flawless.
He set his briefcase down next to her short note;
"I'll meet you in the bedroom…" she wrote.
He smiled and shrugged out of his designer suit jacket,
balled up her note and threw it in the waste basket.
He pulled open the fridge and pushed it shut with his leg.
He laughed softly at another note on the door: "We need eggs."
He poured himself a glass of sweetened ice tea,
took a sip, let out a sigh, content as can be.
He strolled through the house, picking up the clothes that she'd left
all over the floor; her underwear and bra no less.
With a smile he followed the trail of clothes to their room.
The sheets were tangled; the air thick with a strange perfume.
In the corner, a man's jeans and belt that were not his own.
Piled with hers, they were carelessly thrown.
He picked them up, they felt heavy as lead.
He dropped their clothes, in a heap, on their bed.
The truth was there, a truth he refused to digest.
The shower was running; his heart froze solid in his chest.
Coldness embraced him, no amount of heat could ever thaw.
He turned the other cheek, made himself forget what he saw,
turned his back on their laughter, waked out to the car.
They needed eggs.

Glass Eyes

Cool forest trails and wide-open fields
give way to fire place mantles and wounds left unhealed.

Fresh scents on the breeze from the endless, open skies
give way to ceiling fans that bring stale air and old lies.

The rustle of leaves and the call of the birds
give way to the blare of TV and meaningless words.

A calm brown gaze met in the scope of a gun
gives way to a hopeless fear as, shot, he still tries to run.

The sight of the hunter and its sharp silver knife
gives way to nothing more than an ended life.

A creature who knows how cruel humans can be
gives way to a head on the wall and glass eyes that no longer see.

The Weight of the Rain

They walk
bent over,
chin to their chests,
as if it will protect them.

It won't.

The cold soaks them
within seconds,
down to the marrow of their bones.

And now they walk,

hunched,

because they cannot carry the weight of the rain.

The Future Is Ours

The trees scream in the distance and
fall to the ground
like thunder
in July.
As forests
older than the moon
wiser than the tides
are gutted like freshly caught fish.
And the wind whips
wistfully over the new plains
with no leaves or branches to
sway and dance with.
The air thickens,
tastes like cotton
in our mouths
and blankets our tongues.
The sun's gaze
beats down on the poles
burning the glaciers
until they cry for mercy.
We ignore the signs
pretend nothing is wrong,
but even children
cannot play pretend forever.

there is no such thing as silence

the refrigerator hums
as electricity flows
through its veins

the house creaks as it
settles
in its foundation
like a grandfather
settles
in his old leather chair

the wind whips across the window pane
as it goes on its way
with no idea where it's headed
and no memory of where it's been

a heart beats
like a drum
in the distance
buried
in my chest
echoing   -ing   -ing
in my ears

lub-dub--dub   -dub
lub-dub--dub
lub-dub

The sunshine passes
unfiltered
between the frozen limbs
of sleeping trees.
Her light touches my chilled skin
but she's too far away
for me to feel her warmth.
I wonder if the hard earth beneath me
feels as abandoned as I do
as she kisses the horizon
and leaves behind a bleeding sky.

I want to taste
the blue of a
cold winter sky.

I want to feel
the glaring white of the
snow below.

I want to see
the air slip between my
feathers as I soar.

I want to listen to
the sun's love
from above me.

I want to surround myself
with the silence
of the clouds.

I want to fly
higher and higher
until I forget
what the ground looks like.

I wish I were a bird.

The sun slips below the horizon,
disappearing from a violet sky,
as a crow flies straight
toward an old oak tree.
The somber bird perches
on the tallest branch and sits
still as a stone in a dried-up riverbed.
The tree,
fat limbs heavy,
swollen,
saturated with memories
from all the years it has seen,
seems to sigh,
welcoming an old friend home.

Uranus has 21 moons.

Do they all glow?
Do they fight
to be the biggest?
Brightest?
Most beautiful?

Or do they wallow
in each other's shadows?

Do they bicker
like siblings?
Or battle like enemies?
Would they die for each other?
Or for love?

Is our moon lonely?

(4:12 a.m.)
I wonder.

a sleeping forest

a sleeping forest
the echo of a chainsaw
do the trees tremble?

www.ingramcontent.com/pod-product-compliance
Lightning Source LLC
LaVergne TN
LVHW041557070426
835507LV00011B/1144